We thank you Lord,
for those who will kneel here
and glorify your Holy Name.
Amen.

O come, let us worship and bow down,
let us kneel before the Lord, our Maker!
For He is our God;
And we are the people of His pasture,
and the sheep of His hand.

Psalm 95:6-7

Threading

Illustrated by

DONALD ROWLEY

Our Way

How a Needlepoint Project Ended in a New Church
and
33 Daily Meditations by the Needleworkers on Their Verbs

by THE TWINDER-BINDERS

Afterword by
HOLT GRAHAM

The Episcopal Church of the Nativity
Burnsville, Minnesota

Library of Congress Catalog Card Number: 79-65059

ISBN 0-9602848-1-8

Printed by

LAKELAND COLOR PRESS

Brainerd, Minnesota

Dedicated

to

The Glory Of God

and to

Polly McCrea

Dorothy Curtis

Acknowledgments

Thanks go, first and foremost, to our Lord, the Coordinator whose guiding light kept the committee whole as a spiritual body. This unity, which evolved from a simple needlepoint project, proved to be the catalyst for building a church of our own.

Without continued strength and support from the entire parish, we could not have finished the kneelers, much less provided them a permanent home, nor written this book.

To Polly McCrea and Dorothy Curtis, for knowledge and expertise generously offered; to Gretchen Goodman who conceived the idea for doing this book; to Patricia Mertz for help in writing it; to Donald Rowley, the skillful artist; to David Rowley, the sharp photographer; to Lee Kulbitski, the beautiful calligrapher; to Bob McCrea, the generous color specialist; to Bruce Moulton, the patient printer. To Molly Sigal, Joy Yates, Sandy Obarski, Jan Kohout, Meredith Robinson, and Gretchen Goodman who worked on the book project. And to the National Cathedral in Washington, D.C. for inspiration.

To our vicar, Grant Robinson, for his continued and loving support from the beginning. To our friend and Biblical scholar, Holt Graham, for his teaching and gifts.

And, finally, to our long suffering husbands.

Peace,
The Twinder-Binders

Contents

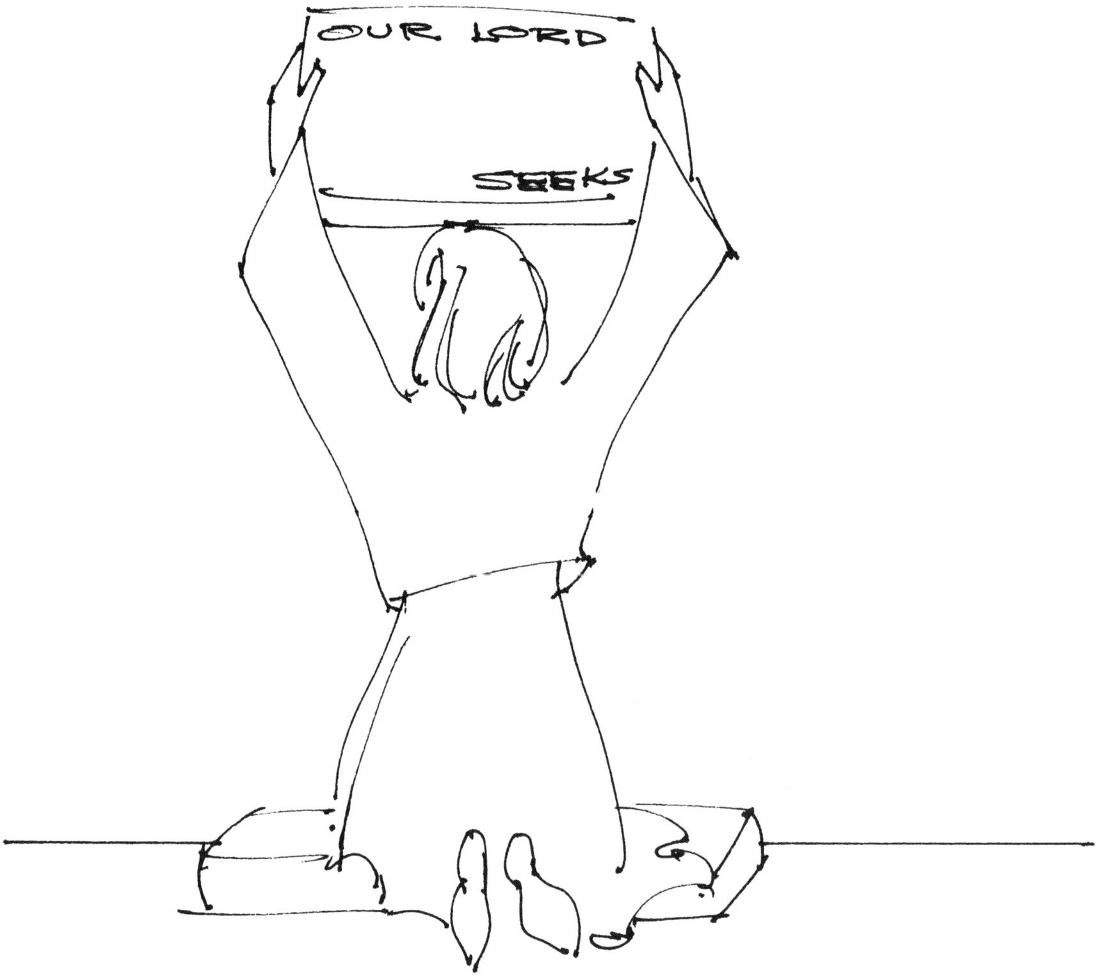

'THESE OFFERINGS ARE ULTIMATELY PEOPLE'

Foreword

We visited a number of beautiful churches and cathedrals when we were in England. One of the things we never failed to admire was the many items of needlepoint. Fine as the work was, there was nothing that could compare with what has been done in this little mission in Burnsville, Minnesota. When I expressed this opinion to Meredith, she said, "You're prejudiced." She's right. I am prejudiced — and I'm proud — and I think I have reason to be both.

Every time I approach the altar area of the Episcopal Church of the Nativity and see those kneelers that the beautiful, dedicated people of our mission have offered, my pride and prejudice grows. There is nothing like these anywhere.

But it is not the fine workmanship that gives them their special quality. I don't see needlepoint when I look at these kneelers. After all, in our technological age, there is probably a machine somewhere that can stitch one. What makes them what they are is not simply pulling a piece of yarn through some 40,000 holes.

The unique quality of these offerings is that they literally come from inside the persons who created them. More than just the sheer labor represented is the offering of the persons and their faith and growth. You can't do something like this without giving of yourself from deep within. You can't do something like this without growing deep within. These offerings are ultimately people, not just stitches. And after all, isn't it us our Lord asks for, and not just our labor?

Grant Robinson, Vicar

About the authors:

The Twinder-Binders joined together three years ago to record the story of their mission's experience. They pursued the details and the unwritten emotions of the forty or more who worked on the project.

Gretchen, Joy, Meredith, Jan, Sandy, and Molly all participated in the kneeler project.

Introduction

We are members of an Episcopal Mission located in a small suburb south of Minneapolis. For fourteen years we worshipped in a rented space.

Then one day in 1974 a member said: "Why don't we make something to beautify this concrete block setting?"

The priest's wife suggested needlepoint communion cushions.

As these 33 beautiful and inspiring kneelers were designed and created by novice needlepointers, a case of "kneeler pride" developed.

"Wouldn't it be nice if we had our own building?" we sighed wistfully. "These kneelers deserve their own sanctuary!"

Thus was launched a project that drew this fledgling parish together. Since Christmas of 1977 we have had our own home with highly original kneelers surrounding the sanctuary. Thus the Episcopal Church of the Nativity, Burnsville, could be called, "the church that kneelers built."

Like all people everywhere, Nativity needed to search out its own identity. In the conception, designing, and developing of the kneelers, we have come a long way in identifying who we are. As we discovered who our Lord was, we found ourselves. So the project has truly been a unifying thread.

In telling our story, it is hoped that other groups will discover their hidden talents and receive encouragement to begin, and the inspiration to complete, their own significant project.

> Having gifts that differ according to the grace given us, let us use them.
>
> Romans 12:6

✠ ✠ ✠

Part I

The Unifying Thread

The Project Story

Only one of us had ever stitched in needlepoint before. So a few took a beginning class from a shop which specializes in custom needlepoint. This tiny nucleus of Needlers, our nickname, taught others.

In our group were men, women and children. The youngest stitchers began their kneelers when they were fourteen. Bruce, Susan and Dorinda chose acolyte cushions depicting Nativity scenes. Chris found time to stitch in her high school senior year and later in college. Who says God is dead on campus?

The variety of interest and backgrounds in our group became a tremendous asset, with many undiscovered talents surfacing.

"Who me? I can't sew, paint OR stitch!" was heard often. But it was followed by, "Well, I suppose I could try."

With a lot of advice and encouragement from people outside our group who had the knowledge and experience we lacked, we began the project in 1974.

A total of about 30 people contributed. Some of those did not actually insert yarn into the canvas, but offered their talents in related areas, such as money raising, art work, canvas preparation and finishing. Many of us stayed throughout the entire project; some simply passed through, because we are basically a transient suburban mission.

When a member moved away, she either gave up her kneeler to another member for completion, or she finished stitching it herself and mailed it back to us.

> For as one body we have many members, and all the members do not have the same function, so we, though many, are one body in Christ, and individually members of one another.
>
> Romans 12:4

Several Minneapolis—St. Paul parishes had completed similar projects, and we studied their finished work as we conceived ours. Shades of red, seen often on our field trips, looked terrific in established churches with dark wood and warm interiors. However, we were not encumbered with existing color schemes — because our hallowed halls were rented.

Our original, optimistic timetable scheduled designing for spring, stitching for summer, finishing for fall, with total completion and dedication for that year's Christmas celebration, 1974!

Several subcommittees were formed in the summer of 1974 so that many procedures could be expedited. After all, we were already behind schedule!

The entire group of Needlers quickly divided into two groups — day stitchers and night needlers — each meeting once a week with several coordinators attending both sessions.

Soon the Blue Book, a large ring notebook, was born to attend all meetings and keep track of landmark decisions. It wasn't until much later we thought of inviting a tape recorder to some meetings.

The Blue Book contains critical information such as the names of stitchers, color mixing formulas for oil paints, alphabet charts, counting methods needed to mark new canvas, plus a few pictures noting progress.

But what came first was the crux of the matter — the decision to make each kneeler original. Meredith, our priest's wife, was to come up with this inspired idea which fired us with enthusiasm.

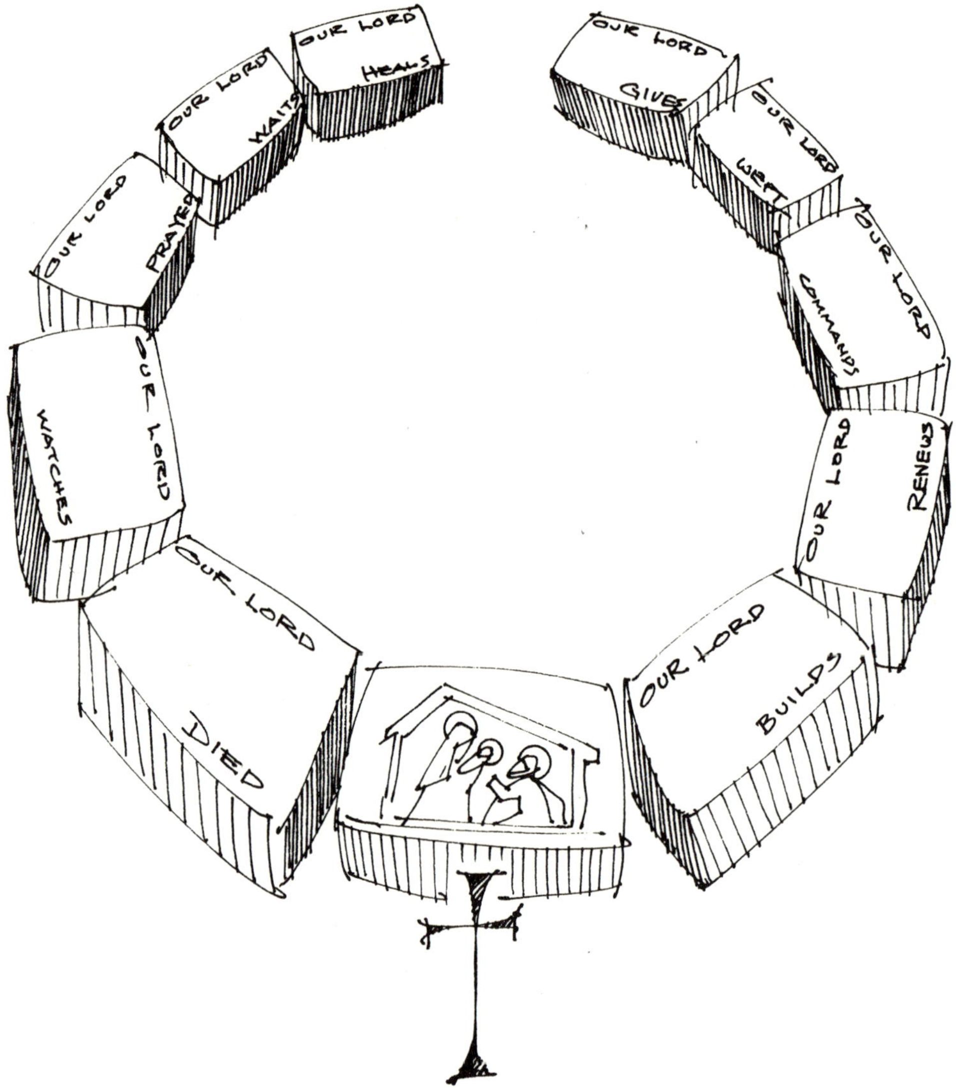

EACH KNEELER WAS TO BE A JEWEL
IN A NECKLACE OF THOUGHTS ABOUT OUR LORD

Each kneeler, we decided, would be different and original — no standard, packaged church designs for us! But we needed a unifying thread to run through them all.

"How would it be," Meredith mused, "if we used the words, 'Our Lord,' followed by a verb describing one of the actions of 'Our Lord' throughout the Bible?"

It would be perfect, we decided. Each kneeler was to be a jewel in a necklace of thoughts about our Lord.

Our priest, Grant Robinson, came up with some 45 action words associated with our Lord: throughout the Old Testament, during His life on earth, and as He lives today.

As potential Needlers became excited about our project, each was given a choice of verbs. A home economist chose "feeds," an airline employee designed "ascended," a North Dakota farm girl designed "renews," and a social activist chose "seeks."

Lee felt the verb "commands" chose her; our Lord commanded Lee to needlepoint the kneeler without her mother's expertise.

Interestingly, the families who chose "creates," "lives," "renews" and "the Holy Family" acolyte cushion were all blessed with additions to their own families.

We discussed whether the verbs to be used should be in the present or the past tense. This brought us to grips with theological questions:

- Does our Lord God still live?
- What does our Lord promise now?
- Did our Lord Christ suffer only during His life here on earth?
- Does our Lord still create in the 20th century?
- Does our Lord still speak to us today?

In the end, only a few verbs were left in the past tense, covering the period of Jesus' lifetime in Palestine. These were "died," "rose," "wept," "suffered," "ascended," "rebuked," and "prayed."

Most of our kneelers are in the present tense because we decided, discovered, or felt convinced that our Lord acts in the here and now.

During this decision process, some of the women, like Sue, went back to their Bibles. Judi took her thoughts to the family dinner table where each of her children gave examples from the Bible on how prayer is answered. Meredith listened to the opinion of the Needlers as the rainbow from the story of Noah was discussed. One week the verb was past tense; a week later it was changed to present tense. But always the unique stamp of the individual persisted.

> "Holy, holy, holy, is the Lord God Almighty, who was and is and is to come!"
>
> Revelation 4:8b

Designing was breaking into reality. Each Needler had to choose a symbol which best represented her verb.

"Our Lord Loves" was probably one of the most difficult to design. Sandy resolved the problem with a very elaborate cross radiating light in the manner of rings radiating from a pebble thrown into a pond — ripples of love.

The kneeler "heals" probably went through the most drastic revisions. It was one of the earliest conceived, and one of the last designed. In the beginning "heals" started with a mended heart, changed to a simple cross, and finally ended with a basket of fruit. A doctor's admonishment to "consider yourself whole" combined with our understanding that when we are healed we are fully healed — our body and our spirit. Such a healing produces the "fruits" of the Spirit — love, joy and peace.

"Our Lord Creates" was originally designed with cute nursery-type animals. But after re-reading Genesis, Sue decided people were the ultimate creation. "Creates" is now designed with simple paper doll type people on a circle to indicate the earth, with satellite rings to represent the universe.

Dea talked with her husband to decide how to illustrate her feelings about the purity and simplicity of "forgives" which she visualized from the priest's blessing.

"Waits" began with no symbol. Then Dorothy designed a sun rising, but it was never completed. Finally, a rose and a bud were chosen.

Besides being novice needlepointers, we did not have an "artist in residence." We worked from library book illustrations, from greeting cards, children's coloring books, and, in one case, a newspaper ad. That's how we came by the symbol for "rebuked" . . . from a newspaper ad which graphically showed a lightning bolt. The newspaper happened to be under a freshly painted canvas. Serendipity?

Friends also helped with designs, as in the case of Bobbie's praying hands, and the clerical kneelers.

Of invaluable assistance was Polly McCrea, owner of a needlepoint shop, the Needle Nest in Wayzata. One of her staff artists drew the designs for the wheat, grape leaves and ferns which appear as backgrounds in 25 kneelers. These three basic forms were drawn and redrawn, turned over, around, and upside down until we had many design variations of our basic leaves, wheat and ferns.

Giving us design problems was the frontal, that wrap-around edge which would be the same on each cushion. We tried samples with "Holy, Holy, Holy," "Shalom," "Alleluia," and Christian fish symbols, finally deciding on Alisee Patee crosses.

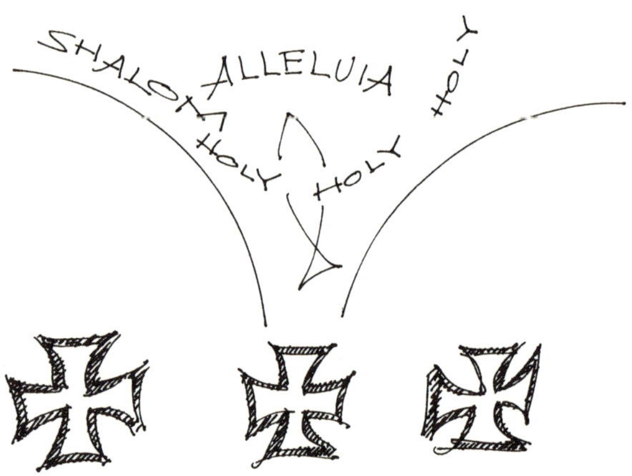

'WE WERE FORCED TO CREATE'

Basically, we found that because we started from zero experience, we were forced to be creative.

Basic to the beauty of the kneelers was the choice of colors. Ours are not the cathedral crimsons nor the regal purples, but bright, contemporary, happy colors in the blue, green and gold range.

Early on we had decided, following Polly's advice, that the extensive background colors would be shades of delft blue. "You'll never tire of these shades," Polly said as she removed several skeins from her shelves. We agreed and ordered 23 pounds of wool all at once so that the dye lots would be the same. This included 3 blues and 2 greens.

After each design was drawn in black and white or with colored crayons, the stitchers went to Polly. A color expert, she often suggested several choices for the symbols, letting each Needler choose her own. For instance, she gave Judi three sets of hues for "abides." She suggested jewel colors for kings and shades of leather and parchment for Joy's Bible. For "feeds" she told Phyllis she visualized a salmon for the fish fed to the multitudes.

Grape leaves, done in two shades of green, form the background design for eleven kneelers. Eight kneelers use green ferns, and six use wheat, done in three shades of gold. These colors, juxtaposed with the background blues, and the bright symbol colors, form a happy rainbow when arrayed around the sanctuary.

In the beginning God created . . .

Genesis 1:1

Conceiving the design was almost easy compared with applying it to the canvas. We realized, though, that these intermediate steps would be very important to a fine finished product.

The group, armed with canvas, rulers, scissors and masking tape, met one day at Gretchen's home. We carefully divided the total amount of canvas and found the most economical way of cutting to minimize waste. We carefully kept track of the "grain" of the bolt by immediately noting with marked masking tape which direction it had been cut from, and therefore, which were the upper and lower, right and left corners.

At this point we masked all edges of each kneeler to prevent raveling. We also noticed "blobs" on the canvas threads caused by knots or by overzealous starching in manufacture. This occurs in all canvas price ranges. We were able to work around them so that the "blobs" were in the margin, not in the canvas center.

The next big step was marking each "hunk" of canvas with the border outline. Sue devised the master plan for finding the exact center and counting the exact number of warp and woof (horizontal and vertical) threads to each margin. The day people brought bag lunches to church, and with good sunshine we began the mind boggling task. Each kneeler had to be counted accurately so that all would be the same when finished.

Onc pcrson rcad instructions while the others in the group, each with a single piece of canvas, counted and marked with yarn ties. Corrections can be made easily with this system. One of our professional resource persons now uses our invented technique for thread counting: use a T-shaped wig pin and draw it slowly over the rows being counted. This "popping" sound assures the brain that what the eyes are seeing and the mouth is saying is really happening.

We found size 12 canvas was easiest for beginners to work on. We could get more detail with size 14, but this project would have lasted three years longer with such fine canvas because it takes so long to see progress on it.

Little did we know at this time, all alphabet charts were designed for 10-mesh canvas. A special subcommittee was formed to study alphabet conversion and shape. After the all-capital style was chosen, Sue, Joy and Sandy compacted the "fat" letters such as "m" and "w" into a usable form. Most of this shaping up was done with actual thread and canvas plus our custom graph paper.

In 1974, even in a large metropolitan area like ours, we could not locate 12 square/inch graph paper . . . so Bob, a dedicated husband, carefully converted four squares into 12.

To teach us how to paint our designs on canvas, Polly McCrea held a workshop at church. She told us that having a meticulously accurate, hand-painted canvas would give novice stitchers confidence. While painting these canvases we chuckled to see the effect of interchanging two stitches. The seagull in "Our Lord Ascended" flew in the opposite direction!

The completed designs, which had been drawn on tissue paper, were oulined on the canvas with needlepoint markers, then painted with oils we mixed ourselves. We used oil paint thinned with Grumtine, to a consistency of heavy cream. We mixed our own colors, each stitching Needler selecting her hues with advice from Polly.

After seeing a slide presentation from the National Cathedral in Washington, D.C., we also decided to initial and date each kneeler. After all if England's Elizabeth, the Queen Mother, signed her contribution, so could we!

During the summer of 1974, Molly worked on a model kneeler to make sure the actual finished product would be as beautiful in reality as in our minds.

We liked what we saw. Our first kneeler "kits" with painted designs on canvas and colorful yarns, were ready for stitching in January, 1975.

THE QUEEN MOTHER SIGNED IT...

...SO COULD WE

We began to see a closer relationship develop among the women of Nativity, and we felt a closer relationship with our Lord. We began to appreciate ourselves and our gifts more and more. As various people showed a preference for one stage of the project over another, we rejoiced over the range of skills we were developing and sharing together. But even with some of us choosing to count threads or to count lettering while others chose to design or paint, each person began to feel a possessiveness about her own canvas. When the design, the painting, and the yarn selection were completed, the time for stitching had arrived. This was a thrilling moment for everyone because we had shared the steps along the way.

RANGE OF SKILLS

We decided to work in two-ply Persian yarn and use basketweave stitches exclusively even though these are among the hardest to learn. But the basketweave offers wearability, and we were creating for ourselves and our posterity. We had read in the Washington Cathedral book, *Stitches for God*, that needlepoint is expected to last a minimum of 200 years.

Working with each other, we shared techniques that made the stitching easier. Often someone would help us over the more difficult spots. Left handers developed their own clique.

Perhaps an expert could detect the slight tension variation in Mary Ann's "Our Lord Rose." Much of this kneeler was stitched in a coronary care unit. As Mary Ann's husband continued to improve, the needlepoint tension relaxed.

Since each stitcher wanted her own canvas to be a perfect offering, she willingly, if not a bit sadly, ripped out mistakes and reworked sections.

Although every step up to this point was shared, the stitching itself was basically a solitary pursuit. Many of us noted that the canvas seemed to share in a dialogue between ourselves and the Word of our Lord Himself.

> **And whatever you do, in word or deed, do everything in the name of the Lord Jesus, giving thanks to God the Father through him.**
>
> **Colossians 3:17**

One October night in 1975 at our rented church, Dorothy Curtis, mother of one of our members and a professional from Bonita Marie's Needlepoint Shop in St. Paul, taught us how to block and mount the cushions which Molly and Judi had stitched.

Later Judi noted that "promises" did not dry on the blocking board properly. The rainbow was definitely "floppy." It needed reblocking. The canvas was blocked again and finally lay flat. That fall, we bought the Delft Blue velveteen which would form the backs of each cushion. It came to $30, astute shoppers that we were.

Then the finishing crew took scissors in hand. Mitred corners, velveteen bottoms, zippers and foam equaled a finished product that is as perfect as humanly possible! Excellent tension, uniform stitching, and quality materials made each needleworker's kneeler as beautiful as the others, regardless of previous expertise.

IT WAS DEFINITELY "FLOPPY"

'WE SUSPECT THE LORD DID SOME PUSHING'

In the fall of 1975, with five embroidered kneelers completed and the rest on the drawing boards, we were well into the project and feeling jubilant.

At a meeting in a parishioner's home, to which we had invited an architect to collect ideas for our new church, Meredith said, "We need space for 33 kneelers."

The architect was incredulous. "Thirty three!" he exclaimed. "Why St. Mark's (the Minneapolis cathedral) doesn't even have 30!"

But we went ahead with plans for 33, one for each year of our Lord's life. Five of these are used in the altar area by the priest, lay readers, and acolytes. These five are specially designed around a Nativity theme, representing our church name.

It was discovered that many stitchers found it difficult to accept the ending of this prayerful experience. Sometimes they moved more slowly as they neared the end. Members of the group had to tease them along. We suspect the Lord did some pushing also.

Throughout the project, we were renewed by small coincidences which pointed to Another who was in charge of us and our efforts, who made us laugh and who quieted us with a power beyond our knowing.

During all the stitching and painting sessions, extreme care had been taken to avoid introducing coffee stains to the canvas. "Waits" was the original sampler and the only canvas to meet a cup running over with coffee.

After completion, three kneelers had close encounters. Bubble gum was found on "lives" and real blood on "died." Wine from the chalice dripped on "gives." Incredibly, all three suffered no permanent damage and are still adorning the chancel of Nativity.

A primary objective had been reached — maximum participation within the parish without sacrificing quality. With the constant guidance, support and challenge of the Holy Spirit, we will complete the project, with the twelfth and final dedication scheduled for January, 1980.

. . . that which we have seen and heard we proclaim also to you, so that you may have fellowship with us; and our fellowship is with the Father and with his Son Jesus Christ. And we are writing this that our joy may be complete.
I John 1:3-4

Our original thought had been to include symbols with each verb so that the Sunday School children who could not read would get a message from the design.

We are so happy that this is what we chose to do, because as we look back, we can see that each needleworker's choice of symbol — and all the research and prayerful thought that ensued — was really the heart of the project.

Struggling not only with the mechanics of stitchery, but most importantly with the message conveyed by the verb, each Needler grew in a personal dimension. In our solitary stitching, we often found ourselves in a meditative moment with our Lord and canvas.

On completing her canvas, each Needler gave some thoughts about her verb and her experience, writing these on cards. Some told why they chose their particular verb. Some described an inner dialogue during the stitching process. These cards were then used by our priest as he prepared his sermon for that particular dedication.

Each time a group of kneelers was finished, we gathered to rejoice. At the altar, each Needler was joined by another parishioner who symbolically represented the assistance of many others.

> **Jesus called them to him, saying,**
> **"Let the children come to me, and do not hinder them; for to such belongs the kingdom of God."**
>
> **Luke 18:16**

THEREFORE DO NOT BE ANXIOUS ABOUT TOMORROW
OUR LORD
LOVES

Kneeler pride cost us some grief as we came to grips with the awful possibility of losing these and other precious possessions.

Our first reaction was disbelief that anyone would steal or even destroy one of our kneelers. Surely the love and effort, freely given by many, would not be wasted! We couldn't conceive of our beloved church without each and every blue kneeler.

After much agonizing over dire possibilities, we faced the fact that yes, we could paint, stitch and finish duplicate kneelers if we had to. But we didn't want to.

We put the problem to our Lord in our prayers . . . and came to understand that with God as the true center of the church, our love should be directed to persons instead of things.

We have gently faced the reality of loss with a new awareness of the overwhelming power and gracious possibilities of Christ's love.

> **Therefore do not be anxious about tomorrow, for tomorrow will be anxious for itself. Let the day's own trouble be sufficient for the day.**
>
> **Matthew 6:34**

✠ ✠ ✠

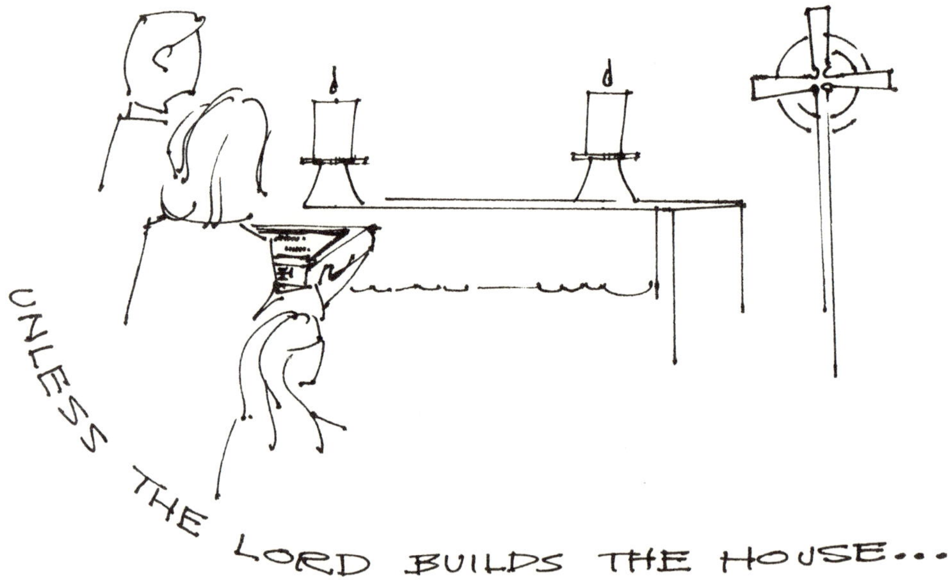
UNLESS THE LORD BUILDS THE HOUSE...

Fittingly, in the Advent Season of 1977, the edifice named The Episcopal Church of the Nativity was dedicated. Each family carried into our new home a church furnishing to symbolize our heritage. Some families carried plants, candlesticks or vestments. But 24 families carried one of our needlepoint kneelers. The dream of our own church building, and the dream of handmade kneelers lining the altar climaxed simultaneously!

> Unless the Lord builds the house, those who build it labor in vain.
>
> Psalm 127:1

WE ARE MORE CLOSELY KNIT AS A COMMUNITY OF CHRISTIANS

One thing we know in our hearts from this experience: We are more closely knit as a community of Christians than we were before the kneeler project.

Our diversity was celebrated each time we remembered those who had the patience to count threads while others contributed an eye for line and color, and still others showed agile fingers for stitching or finishing.

This very diversity taught us the interdependence that St. Paul described so often in his letters to struggling new missions:

> Now there are varieties of gifts, but the same Spirit; and there are varieties of service, but the same Lord; and there are varieties of working, but it is the same God who inspires them all in every one.
>
> I Corinthians 12:4

Now we are surrounded not only with these beautiful works of love, but with the hearts of those who struggled to produce them. The kneelers have grown and so have we . . . because . . .

OUR LORD IS!

Afterword

A nice surprise occurred as I attempted to comply with the invitation to write an afterword for *Threading Our Way*. What kept coming to mind as I read through the narrative was, "To each is given the manifestation of the Spirit for the common good." That is 1 Corinthians 12:7; on the last page of the narrative the quotation is 1 Corinthians 12:4-6!

What St. Paul had in mind as he wrote his succinct phrase *pros to sympheron* ("for the common good") we shall no doubt never know in detail. Some dimensions of what it can mean, however, are woven into this narrative. The common good is common only in its end and outcome: in content and in process it is uncommonly various, diverse, individual. The talents liberated and enhanced by the touch of the Spirit are as diverse as the individuals so touched, and are discovered as they are being exercised.

That has its abiding reflection in the finished kneelers, for each is original and different from every other. Their creators' gifts were, it seems, disclosed to them as they worked toward the common good for which the gifts were bestowed. The choice of a verb was the beginning of a disclosure, the discovery of a clear space, the coming into view of a place native to heart and mind. The choice of a symbol brought into focus and also shaped even as it expressed, the gift evoked and brought to light by the verb.

It is, however, the stitching most of all that reveals the uniquely individual in the common task for the common good. For that is a solitary pursuit in which, to quote St. Paul again, each must bear his or her own burden. It is a task in the doing of which the individual gifts show that they are in turn a composite, for it evokes a whole tapestry of variegated reflections.

For the common good: a simple phrase for a complex reality. The distinctive gifts and talents of each disclosed and developed in choice, in labor, in reflection. In the midst of it all the Spirit bestows His best gift, for as St. Paul says in the chapter next after twelve, the greatest gift is the love that knits together in community — that process so quietly suggested in the words of the narrative about closer relationships. So it is, in a common task, that the church discovers itself in the Lord.

Holt Graham

Part II

The Underlying Thread

33 Daily Meditations by the Needleworkers on their Verbs

Our Lord Creates

Human beings are God's ultimate creation. So the symbol is the universe surrounded by planetary rings, with a family at the center. We visualize the family as the center of God's creation — one of His ways of sustaining us here on earth. In the family, we see the active hand of God in creation from the beginning of the universe through generation after generation of mankind.

Sue

So God created man in his own image, in the image of God he created him; male and female he created them.
Genesis 1:27

The Holy Family

A nativity scene for Nativity — as a new member of our church and community, it definitely helped me feel like I belonged. When co-workers asked about my Christmas decoration, I would launch into my new parish pitch.

Layne

And they went with haste, and found Mary and Joseph, and the babe lying in a manger.

Luke 2:16

Our Lord Gives

What could signify Christ giving His body and blood more than the symbol of the grapes and wheat? To me, the Eucharist means praise, celebration, meditation, love and thankfulness — all in one. So I chose "gives" because of the Sacrament of the Holy Eucharist and its importance to me.

Val

> And he took a cup, and when he had given thanks he said, "Take this . . ."
>
> Luke 22:17
>
> And he took bread, and when he had given thanks he broke it and gave it to them, saying "This is my body."
>
> Luke 22:19

Our Lord Feeds

When I started designing this kneeler, I thought of the feeding of the multitudes with five loaves and two fish. It was indeed a dramatic illustration of feeding the body. As I worked, I felt stronger and stronger that the feeding I desire is the one received from the Lord through the Eucharist.

My prayer is that all who use this kneeler may be truly filled with the love and joy of Christ through his feeding.

Phyllis

There is a lad here who has five barley loaves and two fish; but what are they among so many?

John 6:9

Our Lord Promises

The rainbow is God's promise to be faithful — the glorious colors in the sky after the storm with the arching bow drawing the eyes to the One who promises.

I had two ever-present thoughts during stitching: the common complaint of "Promises! Promises!" with the background echo of "I Never Promised You A Rose Garden." That's the way it is — many days have no rose garden but the great promise of Christ. "Because I live, you live" is consoling and keeps us aware that our Lord promises and is faithful.

Meredith

> And God said, "This is the sign of the covenant which I make between me and you and every living creature that is with you, for all future generations: I set my bow in the cloud . . ."
>
> Genesis 9:12-13

Our Lord Endures

When I first heard the list of verbs available, one spoke to me: "endures." My frequent straying from God . . . He tolerates this and is always there waiting for me to return. His arms outstretched, forgiving my separation. He loves me just as much as if I had never left.

I can't think of a more fitting symbol of His unconditional love than the warm gentle glow of candlelight. The comforting light. His light will not falter. In pain, loneliness and sorrow, as well as in joy and peace, He is with us always — our eternal friend.

Even though I put MY candles out from time to time, I know His light is forever shining its steady glow in loving friendship.

I present this kneeler as my gift of love for a Lord who endures.

Chuckie

O give thanks to the Lord, for he is good, for his steadfast love endures forever.

Psalm 136:1

Our Lord Rebuked

This canvas nearly stitched itself because I didn't want to do it. The negative vibes for punishment were too strong for over a year. Then the positive aspects crept in. Our Lord rebuked waves in the sea and evil spirits — and always corrects with love.

Molly

> And Jesus said, "If you can! All things are possible to him who believes." Immediately the father of the child cried out and said, "I believe; help my unbelief!" And when Jesus saw that a crowd came running together, he rebuked the unclean spirit, . . .
>
> Mark 9:23-25

Our Lord Renews

The kneeler came at a time when I needed to renew many things in my life — from my spiritual renewal to a return to more activities after David's difficult first year. At the same time, another renewal was occurring — that of new life. It was only two months after beginning the project that I found I was pregnant again.

As far as symbols, the hen, rooster, and chicks symbolize for me God's family as well as our own. To me one of our greatest gifts is that of our children — renewal of life at its best, and the constant renewal of our thanks for that gift.

At times it seemed as though I needed to reread the verb because progress was very slow. It was difficult because the children were so small and kept me so busy. But so it is with our faith — mostly hard work and an everyday renewal of our belief and trust.

Mary

> But they who wait for the Lord shall renew their strength, they shall mount up with wings like eagles, they shall run and not be weary, they shall walk and not faint.
>
> **Isaiah 40:31**

Priest's Kneeler

In this kneeler are gathered together all the colors of the other kneelers — of the people — lighted by Christ, the center and the Light of the World.

The manger with the cross behind it is the symbol for the Episcopal Church of the Nativity. The light radiating from the manger moves out to the dawn of Easter in pinks, gold and yellow. Beyond the cross is the green hill of Calvary. Near the cross are blue and purple shades for Mary and her grief.

Opposite the eternal symbol of the Trinity is a town with the Hebrew word, "Shalom," in the sky above.

The Christmas candles stand lighted and waiting for the Gift to be given — the everlasting light.

Meredith

In the beginning was the word . . .

John 1:1

And the word became flesh and dwelt among us, full of grace and truth . . .

John 1:14

In him was life, and the life was the light of men.

John 1:4

Our Lord Calls

I chose "calls" because everywhere I go and in all things I do, I feel the presence of God. He is calling me to be one of His own so that I, too, may share in His joy, peace and happiness.

As God calls to me, so do I call to Him — in my prayers and praise — and I know He will always be there.

Chris

. . . and he called to him his twelve disciples . . .
Matthew 10:1

Our Lord Suffered

When I took the verb "suffered," I must admit I hadn't thought much about Christ's suffering — by choice I guess. I do not choose to think about unpleasantness.

The more I worked on the design and the kneeler itself, however, the more I thought of our Lord's suffering. At first it disturbed me: Couldn't God get His message across to man in another way? Why did the humiliation and death of Christ have to be so drastic and horrible?

The more I thought about these and other questions, the more I came to believe that Christ CHOSE to suffer for us. He did not want to suffer for the sake of suffering — but for our sake, out of love.

In a small way we reflect this choice when we take on the pain of a child or the load of worry or frustration of a friend rather than see them suffer. We can sometimes lighten their suffering with concerned love, but never take it on completely.

Christ DID, however. He suffered in order to give us a view of the complete love that could come only from God.

Phyllis

. . . and plaiting a crown of thorns they put it on his head, and put a reed in his right hand and kneeling before him they mocked him . . .

Matthew 27:29

Our Lord Heals

I chose "heals" because of a special happening in my life. A close relative went blind several years ago. She learned to live with her disability but died suddenly, having loved but never having seen my children. The children and I discussed how lonely we felt. Then their faces brightened, they smiled and said, "Now Dearest can see us!" This thought helped our healing process.

The symbol in this kneeler was fruit, signifying wholeness — the fruits of the Spirit.

Jan

> . . . upon him was the chastisement that made us whole,
> and with his stripes we are healed.
>
> Isaiah 53:5
>
> Now the man who had been healed did not know who it was,
> for Jesus had withdrawn, as there was a crowd in the place.
>
> Luke 5:13

Our Lord Died

During stitching the reality and finality of death by crucifixion took on new significance. Fortunately I knew the end of the story, and that made the reality of the resurrection come closer.

Jean

. . . he said, "It is finished"; and he bowed his head and gave up his spirit.

John 19:30

Our Lord Rose

To me the butterfly has always been one of the most glorious sights in the world. To change from a long, fuzzy, unpretentious, dull worm into that most beautiful creature flitting about is a real miracle of nature.

To realize that this lovely symbol also stands for the resurrection of our Lord was an inspiration. To know that Christ lived, died and rose for us, and that God sent his only Son to love, help, guide and strengthen us is the real inspiration. Could He have done this if His only Son had not risen to be by His side?

Mary Ann

"Do not be amazed; you seek Jesus of Nazareth, who was crucified. He has risen, he is not here . . ."

Mark 16:6

Our Lord Ascended

The bird represents the Holy Spirit. In prayer when we lift up our hearts, the Spirit unites us with God. The grape leaves represent the mystical body.

Gisela

As I complete this kneeler from our new home in Oklahoma, I'm happy that it is finished; but also sad, because it was my last link with Nativity.

Jean

And when he had said this, as they were looking on, he was lifted up, and a cloud took him out of their sight.

Acts 1:9

No one has ascended into heaven but he who has descended from heaven.

John 3:13

Kings

I felt drawn to the three "Kings" because of my association in two productions of "Amahl and the Night Visitors." Initially I thought it would be easy to design because of our church's banner of the kings, which appealed to me. I wanted my kings to look like that. But I was frustrated trying to capture that look. Eventually, after many changes, the kings finally suited me. They looked at peace.

Dorinda

> . . . behold, wise men came from the East to Jerusalem, saying, "Where is he who has been born king of the Jews? For we have seen his star in the East, and have come to worship him."
>
> Matthew 2:1-2

Our Lord Prayed

I believe in the power of prayer — how we pray or where doesn't matter. What does matter is that God knows the sincerity of our prayer and answers with his powerful love. We are human and need his forgiveness.

Bobbie

"I do not pray for these only, but also for those who believe in me through their word, that they may all be one . . ."

John 17:20-21

Our Lord Abides

I chose a tree in winter to represent "abides" . . . because at that time of year you don't know it's alive; but it is, and it's always there, just as the presence of the Lord. He is there and His love abides. The star is for the guiding star of Bethlehem, and the shepherd's crook is from the 23rd Psalm.

The kneeler is a symbol of the strength of the Lord in my life and, hopefully, in the lives of those who kneel here.

Judi

God is love, and he who abides in love abides in God, and God abides in him.

I John 4:16

By this we know that we abide in him and he in us, because he has given us of his own Spirit.

I John 4:13

Our Lord Seeks

When I think of "seeks," I think of Ezekiel 34:12.

"As a shepherd seeks out his flock when some of his sheep have scattered abroad, so will I seek out my sheep — and I will rescue them from all places where they have been scattered on a day of clouds and thick darkness."

We are all, on many days, under clouds and surrounded by thick darkness. With Christ as our model, we are called to follow in His steps — to feed His lambs — to tend His sheep — to feed His sheep. This He said to Simon Peter; but I truly believe He was calling us all to be recipients of His seeking love.

We are sought unceasingly to become living channels of His love. There are limitless ways open to us; through the miracle of surgeon's hands, the careful tenderness of mothers and fathers, the help of all who serve, and the loving concern for our neighbors, be they near or far off.

Edith

"What man of you, having a hundred sheep, if he has lost one of them, does not leave the ninety-nine in the wilderness, and go after the one which is lost, until he finds it?"

Luke 15:4

Our Lord Watches

I believe that our Lord does "watch," knowing what His people think and do; that He gives us freedom to act, but guides us when we seek Him or need Him and that through the passage of time, His will prevails. Our Lord watches for you and me as we dare to watch for Him.

Mary

"Remain here, and watch with me."

Matthew 26:38

Our Lord Wept

I chose "wept" because I could identify with the verb — I'm a weeper. The color of tears is iridescent like water with reflection of all the other colors. There was no question which background to use — grape leaves because the tears showed better against them.

Gretchen

Jesus wept. So the Jews said, "See how he loved him!"
John 11:35-36

Our Lord Commands

God seems to have plans for us that we might not choose on our own. In the beginning I procrastinated. Some gentle prodding and many hints over two years finally produced the beginnings of a design and a painted canvas. I still felt unworthy of so ominous a task. I had looked at "commands" enough times to know that the kneeler would be completed and that I had to do it and no number of excuses were going to alter the fact that I was indeed commanded to complete this kneeler.

Our Lord does command. He cannot be denied. He gets His way. It has been a powerful lesson for me. I will be changed forever just by putting some stitches in a piece of canvas.

Lee

> And he answered, "You shall love the Lord your God with all your heart, and with all your soul, and with all your strength and with all your mind; and your neighbor as yourself."
>
> Luke 10:27

Infant

I remember a small book, "As We Saw It," that our family uses at Advent celebrations. Since the theme was the Nativity story I chose the manger which was on the cover of the book. I had hoped to stitch an acolyte kneeler while I was an acolyte. But we moved to Oklahoma and I couldn't. But at least I made all the decisions for the design.

Susan

And she gave birth to her first born son and wrapped him in swaddling cloths . . .

Luke 2:7

Our Lord Loves

The cross in the center of this kneeler symbolizes the love of God, the circles around the cross stand for the spreading of His love to all the world. For God loves each and every one of us. We are all important to Him.

Sandy

For God so loved the world that he gave his only Son, that whosoever believes in him should not perish but have eternal life.

John 3:16

Our Lord Lives

To me the meaning of the birth and life of Jesus is analogous to the daffodil, one of spring's first and most beautiful flowers. A parallel can be seen in the description of this lovely flower: The sunny trumpeting daffodil heralds spring — a time of new life. It is harbinger of beautiful things to come. It calls out to the earth to begin anew. It is a prelude of an exciting and joyous time of the year, a messenger of life after winter's cold infinite void.

Marcia

It is no longer I who live, but Christ who lives in me . . .

Galatians 2:20

". . . because I live, you will live also."

John 14:19

Our Lord Forgives

Clean, fresh and new is what it feels like to be forgiven. It's not what you were that counts, but what you are — and you are a forgiven person after absolution. I chose a white cross, the perfect symbol of forgiveness.

Dea

And Jesus said, "Father, forgive them; for they know not what they do."

Luke 23:34

Our Lord Answers

The children's Bible story of John the Baptist's birth to very old parents was one form of answer. The cross is another constant reminder of our Lord's answer to our prayer for a savior now at this moment. The shepherd reciting the 23rd Psalm reminds us that He will answer us. These symbols come from an awareness that our Lord always answers in the present tense.

Judi

. . . and the dove came back to him in the evening, and lo,
in her mouth a freshly plucked olive leaf; so Noah knew . . .
Genesis 8:11

"Ask, and it shall be given you . . ."
Matthew 7:7

Our Lord Teaches

There was no question of a symbol. It had to be the Bible. Every time we enter a church, the Bible is displayed. And at every service, it is read from. What we know about God or have been taught about God finds its source in that book.

Joy

And when Jesus finished these sayings, the crowds were astonished at his teaching, for he taught them as one who had authority.

Matthew 7:28-29

Our Lord Speaks

"Speaks" was probably the first and easiest to design. We copied it from a photo depicting Mary Magdalene's hair, and turned it upside down! The design movement was instantly appealing. Later, as I worked the kneeler, the visions of the Old Testament "burning bush," ordination, speaking in tongues, and the charismatic movement entered my thoughts as I stitched.

Molly

God called to him out of the bush, "Moses, Moses!"
Exodus 3:4

Animals

I enjoyed stitching my kneeler since it was quite a challenge. It did get frustrating at times and would have gone faster except for changes I had to make in design. I wondered why the baby was not visible in the manger. If there'd been room at the Inn, I wouldn't have had so much trouble with the camel's legs or the color of the stable wood.

About the baby in the manger . . . there's about as much evidence of the baby in the manger as there is of us teenagers in church.

Bruce

. . . and laid him in a manger, because there was no place for them in the inn.

Luke 2:7

Our Lord Builds

Our Lord builds a community, a community of believers in the kingdom of God. He adds to it and strengthens it each day. He builds his church — not only the structures themselves, but the family or community of believers inside. Thus, on my kneeler for "builds" I have chosen a family of cardinals, three birds on evergreen branches.

Anne

"and on this rock I will build my church . . ."

Matthew 16:18

Our Lord Washes

I originally chose "washes" because of the design possibilities of the seashore adorned with shells of beautiful shapes and colors. Surely the scallop, symbolic of baptism, and the sand dollar, symbolic of death and resurrection with its nail wounds and Easter lily, would be included. As I grew with my kneeler, the cleansing and forgiving aspect of washes developed. Would our Lord wash away my feelings of guilt at procrastinating and being so slow to begin? He seems to wash the whole world at its seashores.

Gretchen

. . . and when he came up out of the water, immediately he saw the heavens opened and the Spirit descending upon him like a dove . . .

Mark 1:10

Our Lord Waits

The thought of waiting is inextricably bound to the ideas of expectation and patience. Who has not watched a rose grow from tender shoots in the spring to beautiful fulfillment in the summer? One feels a sense of expectation as the bud appears, and must have patience to allow it time to unfold in complete beauty.

Our Lord has expectations of each of us, and He has the loving patience to allow each of us time to find our own unfolding purposes.

Shann

Therefore the Lord waits to be gracious to you; Therefore he exalts himself to show mercy to you. For the Lord is a God of justice; Blessed are all those who wait for him.

Isaiah 30:18

Our Lord Is

In the New Testament, as commonly in Greek, the word "is" is not there — it's "understood," as the grammarians say. Indeed it is: His Lordship implies his Being.

We children of time, however, need a bit more help than that, help kindly supplied in Hebrews 13:8, "Jesus Christ is the same yesterday, today, and forever." The very tenses of Advent! He is the One therefore in whom we vest our hope.

Forever: for the future is in the hands of the Lord of time, who will bring to completion and fulfillment what he has begun in us, the life that is sustained by faith and the work inspired by love.

Today: for his is the Presence made known to us by the loving pressure of the Holy Spirit upon our spirits. It is not the same for all of us, nor need it be. (None of us qualifies as one of God's mistakes!) For some, the gentle insistence of the Spirit makes the Lord Jesus known as a vividly personal Presence: comforter and guide, judge and companion. For others he is made known in the form of an irresistable conviction of the everlasting importance of truth and justice and mercy, of fidelity and integrity, of the eternal significance of love. No matter which way — Jesus is made known, and known as the Lord who *is.*

Yesterday: herein is the distinctiveness of Christian and biblical hope. Earthly hopes look to the future only: ours embraces the past as well. For the Lord who eternally *is* brings our yesterdays into the present to be healed and to heal, to be redeemed and to redeem. It is in this hope that we read and ponder the Bible, the first great chapter in the story of our common yesterday. The Spirit of the Lord brings that story to life in our present, redeeming the past, to "stablish, strengthen, settle us" for the service of the Lord in the unending present of his Presence.

Holt Graham

We have stitched the thousand stitches
of the many colors in these kneelers, Lord.

We have questioned our abilities as we proceed.

We have only known that we must work with care...
that the stitches chosen
formed a woven piece of fabric
to be used by those we love
and by strangers... yet to love.

The hours we spent
with paint and brush,
with needle and thread,
with each other around a table,
were brightened by the thoughts
of children's lighted faces
as they recognized the pictures
we created.

The canvas held the threads in place
as we stitched each painted intersection,
just as you, dear Lord, hold us in place
as our lives fill, too,
with threads of every hue.

And as we stitched and worked the colors
through our own lives' dark and weary hours,
we offered them to you, Our Lord,
these softly woven threads,
for those precious moments
when we, your children,
kneeling here,
would receive your power
your life
your love
at your Holy Table.

Nativity, Burnsville
December, 1975
Meredith Robinson

Financing and Costs

In April of 1974, with the help of a loan from the Bishop's Committee, we took the plunge and ordered 23 pounds of yarn. This only included the basic background blues and greens.

Our original estimate was that each kneeler would cost about $10 but we needed close to $19 in the end.

It was at this point we realized we needed some fund raising ideas. Anonymous contributions had been our "seed money;" but we needed so many materials now that the work was going in earnest.

One of our members, Kay, maintaining that she could never become a stitcher, offered her fund raising talents in organizing a spring style show of handmade fashions and antique wedding dresses. We also organized parish housewares parties, garage sales, bake sales, and plant sales. Our project suddenly jumped out of the red. But we still minded our pennies.

Keeping the budget in mind, we recycled the stuffing of the faded green cotton kneelers that had served us for so many years.

We designed, painted, stitched, blocked, finished, and stuffed each kneeler ourselves. Had we just done the needlepoint, leaving the designing and finishing charges to a professional shop, the cost would have been much more. Instead we created quality, original, handcrafted items for a most reasonable price.

Do you need professional guidance?

We Needlers agree that it is important to establish a relationship with a needlepoint shop. An amateur doesn't know how to measure yarn or how much to order. While reference books can give you an idea for gauging the quantity for large areas, how do you know how many strands go into a lightning bolt, for instance? If you don't order enough, you may not be able to match shades later in what may be different dye lots.

The professionals at the shops really know how to make materials determinations. They just measure by thumb — feel it — count the number of thumbs, and come up with a quantity measure.

We relied on professionals for color help, too. Once you have established rapport with a shop like Polly's Needle Nest, you can continue your business by mail, if necessary. You could send the tissue-paper pattern with instructions like "Please send us four shades of lavender for lightning." Or, "Please send us samples of lightning colors."

Then you can made your color selections and order by mail. File the snips of yarn you have decided on, along with the pattern. It would also be helpful to know a color number or to have a copy of a color chart from the shop.

A professional's expertise also helped us over a few hurdles where we didn't want to make critical judgments of each other's ideas. We simply took the alternatives to Polly for a decision. And Polly also provided the encouragement to finish what we had started.

Needleworkers And Their Verbs

First Dedication	**Thanksgiving Season 1975**	**December 14, 1975**
Val Nordin	. . . Gives	
Molly Sigal	. . . Speaks	
Phyllis Rowley	. . . Feeds	
Gretchen Goodman	. . . Wept	
Judi Hornbacher	. . . Abides	
Second Dedication	**Easter Season 1976**	**Palm Sunday April 4, 1976**
Meredith Robinson	. . . Promises	
Rev. Grant Robinson*	. . . Died	
Jean Cleek		
Judi Hornbacher	. . . Answers	
Dea Haight	. . . Forgives	
Marcia Gowling	. . . Lives	
Third Dedication	**Thanksgiving Season 1976**	**November 28, 1976**
Mary Ann Ober	. . . Rose	
Mary Heltsley	. . . Watches	
Fourth Dedication	**Easter Season 1977**	**May 1, 1977**
Joy Yates	. . . Teaches	
Meredith Robinson*	. . . Priest's Kneeler	
Judi Hornbacher		
Edith Hatch	. . . Seeks	
Fifth Dedication	**Pentecost Season 1977**	**Stewardship Sunday October 10, 1977**
Sue Kempe	. . . Creates	
Bob Kempe		
Jan Davis*	. . . Holy Family	
Layne Lindquist		
Dorinda Yates*	. . . Calls	
Chris Ober		
Gisela Burley*	. . . Ascended	
Jean Cleek		

Sixth Dedication	**Pentecost Season 1977**	**November 13, 1977**
Molly Sigal	. . . Rebuked	
Lee Kulbitski	. . . Commands	
Phyllis Rowley	. . . Suffered	
Jan Kohout	. . . Heals	
Seventh Dedication	**Thanksgiving Day 1977**	**November 24, 1977**
Chuckie Pattie	. . . Endures	
Eighth Dedication	**Easter Season 1978**	**April 9, 1978**
Iris Evans*	. . . Kings	
Dorinda Yates		
Ninth Dedication	**Pentecost Season 1978**	**November 12, 1978**
Sandy Obarski	. . . Loves	
Mary Ellingrud	. . . Renews	
Tenth Dedication	**Epiphany Season 1979**	**February 25, 1979**
Jan Davis*	. . . Animals	
Bruce Goodman		
Bobbie Popilek	. . . Prayed	
Eleventh Dedication†	**Easter Season 1979**	**May 13, 1979**
Susan Cleek*	. . . Infant	
Jeanne Marsh		
Twelfth Dedication†	**Pentecost Season 1980**	
Gretchen Goodman	. . . Washes	
Anne Malone	. . . Builds	
Judi Hornbacher*	. . . Waits	
Shann Valentine		

* Designer; Stitcher follows
All other kneelers were designed and stitched by one Needleworker

† These kneelers are in the stitching stage, Spring 1979

Additional copies of *Threading Our Way* may be ordered through the
Episcopal Church of the Nativity, 2400 W. Highland Dr., Burnsville, MN 55337
We invite your comments and responses
that we might share in your joy.